How to Be Popular

by Margot Shales

illustrated by Tamara Petrosino

Harcourt

Orlando   Boston   Dallas   Chicago   San Diego

Visit *The Learning Site!*

www.harcourtschool.com

"This is the most ridiculous thing I've ever seen!" Suzy Hsu announced to no one in particular. She was standing in the hall next to the main office, glaring at something that had been posted on the bulletin board. Other students were milling around in the hall before school began.

Just then, Margaret Jace wheeled up in her chair.
Margaret was one of the most active students in the school.
In fifth grade an article about her had appeared in the *Star
News.* The article called her a "student for the new millen-
nium." Margaret had insisted the reporter not mention her
physical disability, telling him, "That's just not important. I'm
a person like anyone else; this wheelchair is just how I get
around." Margaret's down-to-earth attitude made her one of
the most admired students in the school.

"What's so ridiculous?" Margaret asked, and then she saw
what Suzy was looking at: a construction-paper graph that said: "WHO IS MOST POPULAR? CAST YOUR VOTE! *Place your vote in the ballot box below. We'll post your nominee and the number of votes he or she receives on this chart. The winner gets to write the introduction to the year-book and receives $100 for the local charity or cause of his or her choice!"* Margaret looked at the graph and shook her head.

CAST YOUR VOTE!

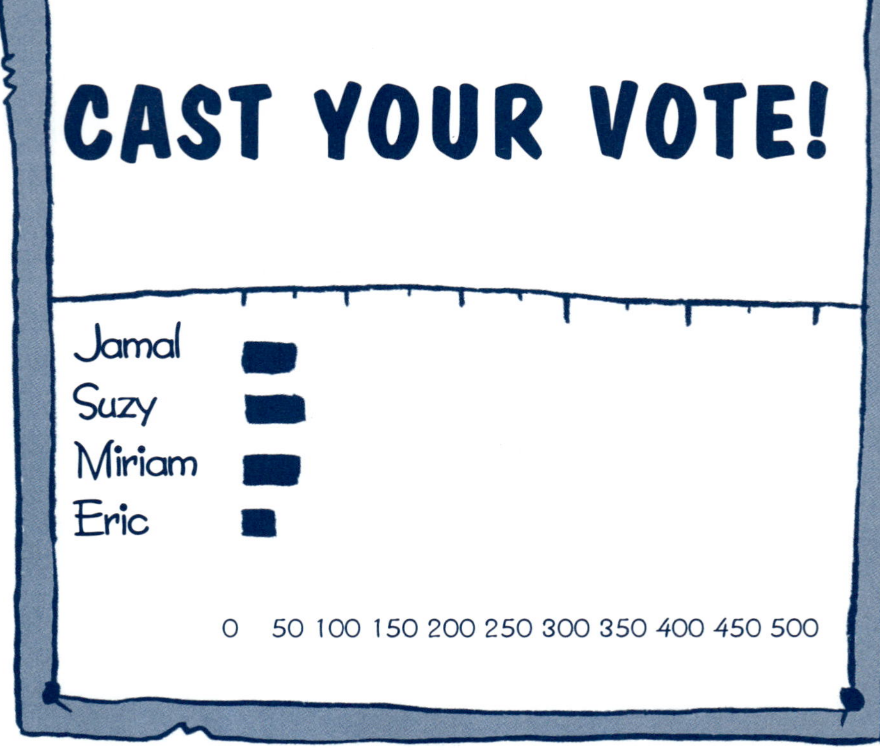

"Oh, that silly thing. Ridiculous doesn't begin to describe it." Margaret read the names on the chart. "Hey, did you read this graph? You're leading the vote."

"So what?" Suzy shook her fists at the chart and then turned to Margaret. "I'm leading because I'm the student council representative for the sixth grade. That's all." It was true: Suzy was remarkably sharp and articulate; she always presented her classmates' requests and concerns with elo-quence—and she usually got results. She was a natural-born leader, and she put her skills to good use.

Suzy bristled now while looking at the graph. "The whole idea of this popularity contest is just plain wrong. I mean, what does it really mean to be 'popular' anyway? Why is it such a big deal?"

Margaret smirked. "Well, I for one do *not* consider being voted 'Most Popular' a big deal. You don't see my name up there, do you?"

"Exactly my point," Suzy said. "You do more for this school in a week than most of the kids on this chart have done in their entire lives. You help with fund-raisers for the soccer team and the basketball team—"

"Yes, and I'm in chorus, drama club, and on the debate team," Margaret added, laughing.

"Right. You're well liked because you're so nice and smart and funny. In fact, I'd guess you're one of the most popular students in this school!" Suzy angrily stabbed at the chart with her index finger. "I'd like to cross *my* name off of that graph; or better yet, I'd like to cast a vote to have the thing thrown into the garbage!"

The bell rang, and the kids in the hall rushed to first
period and the beginning of the school day.

Margaret grinned. "You know, there's more at issue here
than just a popularity contest. We ought to make sure everyone really thinks about the whole notion of popularity."

Suzy raised an eyebrow. "What are you planning?"

Margaret spun her wheelchair away. "I'll tell you later.
Let me check out the school district's ordinance on this first.
See you at lunch."

When the lunch bell rang, Suzy marched straight to the cafeteria, eager to hear Margaret's plan. She spotted Margaret sitting at her usual spot at the corner table, but Margaret wasn't participating in the gossip and joking with the other kids; instead, she was scribbling busily in her notebook.

"OK, Margaret," Suzy said, sitting down on a bench. "What's up?"

Margaret slid her notebook over to Suzy. "Here's our agenda," she said, pointing. "We need to get to work right away if we're going to get enough votes to win this thing."

Suzy checked out the list of "Action Items."

"Slogans?" she asked, confused. "Campaign posters? I don't get it. And who on earth is Misty Wree?" Suzy handed the notebook back to Margaret.

Margaret practically beamed. "Oh, Misty Wree is the sweetest, funniest, kindest, most responsible, and soon-to-be most popular individual in the entire school."

Suzy shook her head. "Sounds like nobody I know."

Margaret chuckled. "Exactly. Misty's nobody. Our candidate doesn't exist."

Suzy laughed out loud. "You want to nominate an imaginary person?"

"Why not? If our school wants to run a popularity contest, then there is nothing to stop us from showing everyone what kind of person a true winner would be."

Suzy looked around at her friends and classmates who were all happily eating lunch. "Won't people be mad at us?"

Margaret shrugged. "Some of the other nominees might be mad, but I think most of the kids in the school will enjoy it." She closed the notebook and slid it into her pack. "Vice Principal Gordon might think it's strange, too, but there's not a whole lot he can do about it. I've checked out the school district's rules, and running a nonexistent person in a student vote is not among a violation of school policy, so we're fine there."

Suzy smiled. "If we win, we can use the prize money for some needy group or to help with library funding. That way, everybody gets something."

"My thoughts precisely," Margaret said, becoming all business. "Now all we have to do is get people to vote for Misty Wree. Can you come over tonight?"

"I'll be at your house at seven," Suzy said.

"Effective right now," Margaret said, "Operation Misty Wree begins."

The next morning, students arrived at school to find posters taped to walls, tacked to trees, and hung from ceilings in every classroom. There were as many different slogans as there were posters. "Misty Wree or Miss Out!" proclaimed one. "Misty Wree Is All You Can Imagine!" read another.

On the bulletin board by the ballot box, a poster read: "Vote for Misty Wree and Find Out How to Be Popular!" Between the two posters, the graph had already been updated: Misty Wree was ahead by more than a dozen votes.

The school was buzzing with rumors by lunch. Who was Misty Wree? Why was Misty's true identity a secret? "It isn't fair at all," Miriam Ashford complained to Suzy. "Why would kids vote for someone they don't even know? They're just throwing their vote away!" Miriam was upset because she was running second to Misty Wree.

Vote for
Misty Wree and
Find Out
How to Be
Popular!

The next morning Suzy and Margaret were excited. Once a week, Suzy read the announcements over the intercom, and today was her turn.

Suzy began, "Today we have an extra-special announcement. It seems that one of the nominees for the popularity contest left a message in the office and asked that it be read to you. Here is that message: 'What is popularity? What makes someone popular? I don't think we should compete with each other over popularity. I *do* think popularity should come naturally from being the best person you can be, even if it's not always being what others call 'cool.' Being the best I can be means never being conceited. It means talking to my classmates and being their friend anytime—not just when it's convenient. It means liking all kinds of people and respecting their differences, too. I hope you'll consider my definition of popular when you cast your vote. Signed, *Misty Wree.*'"

Moments later, the intercom crackled. "Attention, students. This is Vice Principal Gordon speaking. A team of pranksters has targeted the popularity contest with a campaign for someone named Misty Wree." Laughter rippled through Mrs. Garnes's classroom, where both Margaret and Suzy had English class. "I would like to request that students not vote for this Misty Wree character, or I'm afraid I will have to postpone this contest."

"That seals it," Margaret said, satisfaction thick in her voice. "We're sure to win now."

"What are you talking about?" Suzy said, taking her seat in class. "If Misty Wree gets the vote, the contest is postponed."

"That won't matter. What matters is that Vice Principal Gordon has requested that everyone not vote for Misty. You know what that means."

Suzy thought for a second, and then slowly smiled. "That

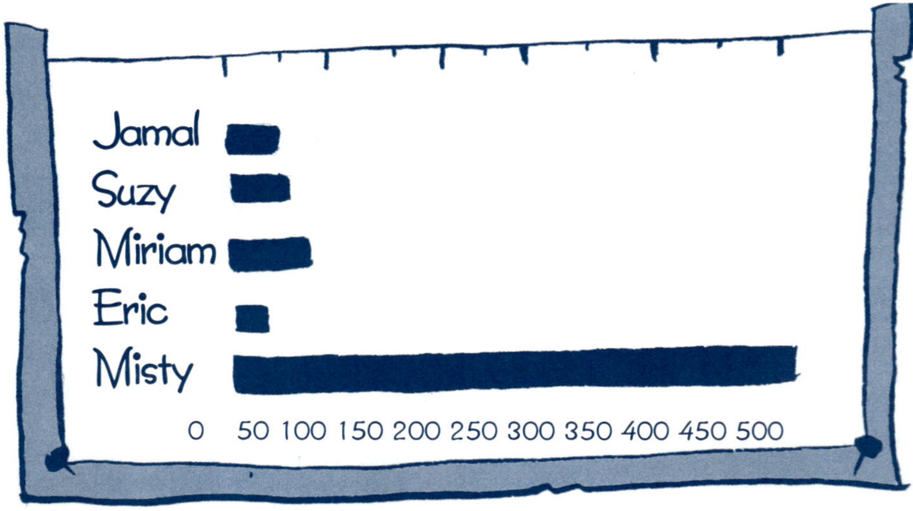

means everybody is going to vote for our candidate."

"Exactly!" Margaret said. She and Suzy shook hands.

By the next morning, Misty Wree had more than 70 percent of all votes cast. The kids in charge of the contest posted the new totals at every class break. A crowd gathered between bells, and every vote given to Misty Wree was met with hoots and claps. By the time lunch rolled around, Misty Wree had 472 votes. The next closest person was Miriam, with 47 votes. Everyone expected Vice Principal Gordon to postpone the contest as he had promised—everyone, that is, except for Margaret and Suzy.

They were picking their way through lunch, a mixture of rice and beans and yellow tortillas. Margaret checked her watch. "Right about now Vice Principal Gordon should be getting a call from the reporter who wrote that story about me for the *Star News*," she said.

Suzy turned to her friend, shocked. "What have you done?" she asked.

"Nothing bad! Come on, you know me better than that." Margaret looked down and grinned into her lunch tray. "I just thought this Misty Wree story might be worth some coverage in a local paper."

"I don't suppose this reporter knows about Vice Principal Gordon's plan to postpone the contest?" Suzy said.

"He might know something about that—and he might also know something about the school district's policy when it comes to officials interfering with student contests."

Suzy shook her head and whistled. "You are one devious person, Margaret."

"Just this once I'll take that as a compliment," Margaret said, and took a bite from a soggy taco.

Everyone waited for Vice Principal Gordon to speak over the intercom and announce the end of the contest. Fourth period passed quietly. Fifth period passed without incident. There were five minutes left in sixth period when Mr. Colin finished his lesson on the Crusades. "Well," he said, "we only have a few minutes left in this period, and you're all staring at the intercom. Are you waiting for Vice Principal Gordon to speak? Does anyone want to talk about the popularity contest? Why do you think people are voting for Misty Wree?" He leaned against his desk at the front of the class. Suzy and Margaret studied their desks.

One student raised his hand. "I think everyone is voting for Misty because Vice Principal Gordon told us not to." Everyone laughed. Then the boy added, "Also, the message we heard shows that Misty doesn't believe in being mean."

"Frank's right," a redheaded girl in the front row chimed in. "Misty Wree isn't disrespectful or rude to people just because they're not 'cool.'"

A tall boy from the back said, "Yeah, Misty doesn't make fun of anyone."

Mr. Colin nodded. "Who do you think Misty Wree really is?"

The boy who had spoken first raised his hand again. "We all know Misty's not real," he said, "but Misty Wree is the kind of kid who deserves to be popular."

Another girl said, "I'd rather cast a vote for someone who isn't real than for someone who I know is not always so nice. At least the fake person won't snub me in gym."

There was a murmur of agreement. Mr. Colin stood up again. "Well, we learned one thing from this popularity contest."

"What's that?" the tall boy asked.

"It seems we all agree: Being popular is not a goal in itself; it's a reward for being the kind of friend that each of us would like to have." He looked at his watch. "Class dismissed."

Misty Wree's acceptance speech was delivered to Vice Principal Gordon by U.S. mail.

I would like to thank my classmates for their votes. In return, I'd like to donate the prize money to the library fund. That way all students can share in the prize. As for the introduction to the yearbook, here is my suggestion:

> "There is none so wealthy as he who counts his friends first."—Anonymous
> Thank you, friends!
> Sincerely,
> Misty Wree

The story broke the next day. The *Star News* ran it on the front page. The headline read "MISTY WREE" WINS STUDENT POPULARITY CONTEST.

Margaret showed the article to Suzy before stuffing it into her backpack. "I wonder if anyone will ever learn who Misty Wree really is?" she asked.

"I don't know," Suzy answered. "I suspect Misty will always be a…mystery!"

The two friends looked at each other and then burst out laughing.